Howard B. Wigglebottom
Learns About Bullies

Written by
Howard Binkow

Illustrated by
Susan F. Cornelison

Written by: Howard Binkow
Illustrated by: Susan F. Cornelison
Book design by: Tobi S. Cunningham

Thunderbolt Publishing
We Do Listen Foundation
www.wedolisten.com

This book is the result of a joint creative effort by Ana Rowe and Susan F. Cornelison.

Gratitude and appreciation are given to all those who reviewed the story prior to publication.
The book became much better by incorporating several of their suggestions.
Jodi Allen, Rhonda J. Armistead, Karen Binkow, Martie Rose Binkow, Deborah Cochran, Leonie Deutsch, Sandra Duckworth, Susan Eden,
Lillian Freeman, Kimberli Garretson, Jan Marie Guinn, Martha Gutierrez, Kerry Haar, Amy Hamilton, Sherry Holland, Tracy Mastalski,
Jennifer Meyer, Cynthia Paonessa, Teri Poulos, Chris Primm, Shelly Rubenstein, Laurie Sachs, Mimi C. Savio, C. J. Shuffler, Nancey Silvers,
Gayle Smith, Paula Spector, Phyllis Steinberg, Joan Sullivan, Rosemary Underwood, and George Sachs Walor.

Teachers, librarians, counselors and students at:
Bossier Parish Schools, Bossier City, Louisiana
Charleston Elementary School, Charleston, Arkansas
Del Norte Elementary, Roswell, New Mexico
Glen Alpine Elementary, Morgantown, North Carolina
Golden West Elementary, Manteca, California
Iveland Elementary, St. Louis, Missouri
J.J. Mulready School, Hudson, Massachusetts

Meadows Elementary School, Manhattan Beach, California
Patterson Primary School, Beaver Falls, Pennsylvania
Payneville Elementary, Payneville, Kentucky
P.S. 7 Queens, Elmhurst, New York
VAB Highland Oaks Elementary, North Miami Beach, Florida
Walt Disney Magnet School, Chicago, Illinois
Westerville City School, Westerville, Ohio
West Navarre Primary, Navarre, Florida

Special thanks to my family for their ideas and support.

Printed in China

ISBN 978-0-9715390-6-8

First Printing

This book belongs to

_____

Sunday night, Howard B. Wigglebottom could not fall asleep. He was very scared.

He could hear a little voice in his head,

Be **Brave**, Be **Bold**, a **teacher** must be **told**.

He knew that tomorrow morning he would once again come face to face with the scary . . .

5

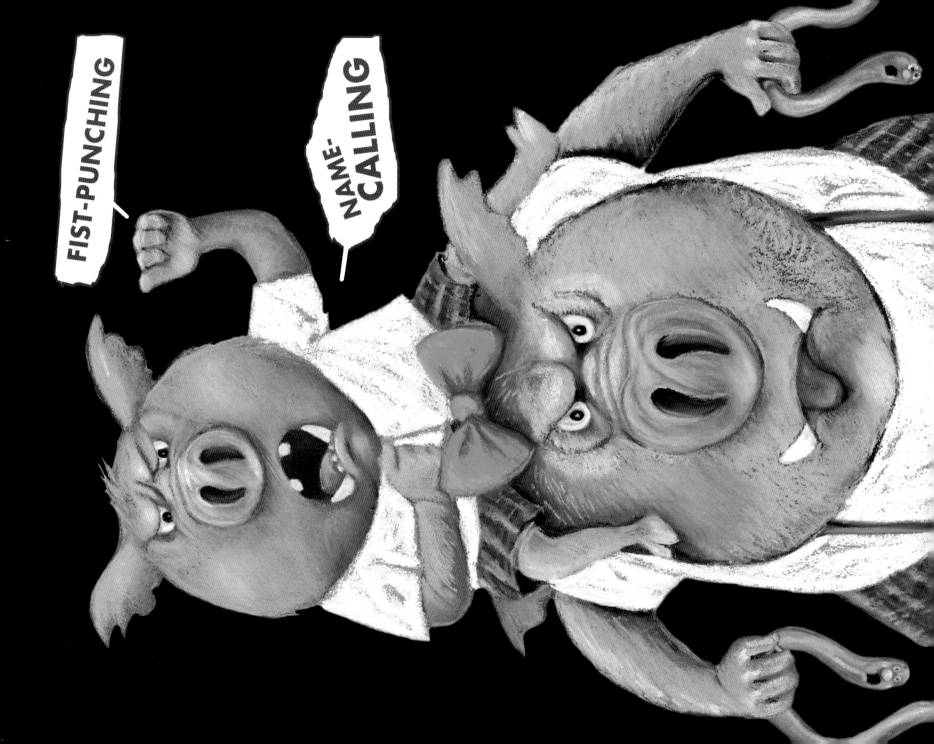

TONGUE-WAGGING

WORM-WHIPPING

FOOT-STOMPING

SNORTON TWINS!

The Snorton twins were, you guessed it, "push you down, steal your lunch, make you eat worms"—the worst kind of bullies . . .

That is . . . when no teacher was looking, of course.

The Snortons felt big and important when they made others feel small and scared. Howard was tired of feeling small and AFRAID all the time.

The little voice in his head said again

Be **Brave**, Be **Bold**, a **teacher** must be **told**.

Howard didn't tell anyone. He was too afraid of being called a tattletale or a snitch. Even worse, he was scared about what the Snorton twins might do to him.

Be Brave, Be Bold, a teacher must be told.

On MONDAY Howard thought, "I will wear my cloak that makes me invisible.
When I walk right past them, they will never see me.
I'll be okay. I'll be safe."

But on Monday, the Snorton twins bullied him and ate his lunch.

Be Brave, Be Bold, a teacher must be told.

On TUESDAY Howard thought, "I will wear my special shoes. I will run like the wind high above the trees. The Snortons will never catch me. I'll be okay. I'll be safe."

15

But on Tuesday, it was not very windy.
The Snorton twins bullied him, ate his lunch,
AND took his shoes.

Be Brave, Be Bold, a teacher must be told.

On WEDNESDAY Howard thought, "I will wear my jacket which transforms me into ROBORABBIT with super powers. I'll twirl and hurl them up into outer space. I'll be okay. I'll be safe."

17

But on Wednesday, the Snorton twins bullied him, ate his lunch, and took his jacket.

Be Brave, Be Bold, a teacher must be told.

On THURSDAY Howard thought, "I will wear my funny hat and be Howard the Hilarious, Mr. Funny Bunny. I will use my quick wit and make them like me.
I'll be okay.
I'll be safe."

But on Thursday, the Snorton twins didn't think
he was all that funny or smart. They bullied him,
ate his lunch, and took his hat.

20

By Friday, Howard was
hungry, tired, and out of
ideas. He decided he would
give the twins whatever they
wanted and just try not to get hurt.

21

On the way to school, Howard overheard the twins arguing and fighting.
"Give me the shoes and the jacket! You said I could wear them." Shouted
Norton Snorton.

"No I didn't. Here, take the hat, you stubby legged short boy"
yelled his sister.

"I'm not short!" Norton Snorton yelled back,
standing on his tiptoes.

"Yes, you are!" she yelled back, puffing out her chest, hands on hips, looking down on her brother.

The Snorton twins puffed and puffed their chests soooOOOO huge that they floated up in the sky like balloons.

Howard watched in amazement as the two drifted away. He could barely hear them calling each other names as he skipped all the way to school.

Okay, okay. Howard's imagination DID get the best of him. On Friday, what REALLY happened was the Snorton twins beat each other up, and they didn't notice Howard at all. By the time he got to school, Howard knew what he had to do, for his sake and for the Snortons.

The voice in his head had been right all along.

Be **BRAVE**, Be **BOLD**, My **TEACHER** Must Be **TOLD**.

And so Howard told his teacher,
who told the Principal,
who told Mr. and Mrs. Snorton.

On Friday night while the Snorton twins were in BIG, BIG, BIG TROUBLE and learning an important lesson, Howard snuggled into bed and whispered softly to himself,

"I WAS brave and bold when my teacher was finally told. I AM okay, I AM safe."

Then he drifted off into a deep, peaceful sleep.

Howard B. Wigglebottom Learns About Bullies
Lessons and Reflections

Bullies

★ If another kid scares you, hurts you, calls you bad names and says bad things about you, makes you do things you don't want to do, tell you who you can or cannot speak to, or if another kid is stealing or breaking your toys and your things, YOU ARE BEING BULLIED!

★ YOU NEED TO TELL A TEACHER RIGHT AWAY! If that doesn't work, you need to tell the principal or a trusted adult.

★ Telling is the right thing to do even if you're afraid or if a big kid or a group of kids are threatening you and warning you not to say anything. If you don't tell, things might get worse. TELLING IS NOT WRONG OR BAD. IT'S THE BEST THING TO DO! BE SMART, BRAVE AND SAFE. TELL A TEACHER RIGHT AWAY!

★ Most of the time, trying to avoid,

  ignore

  joke around or

  have words with the bullies

  WILL NOT WORK.

★ Howard tried many different ways to stop the bullies, but nothing worked until he told his teacher. YOUR TEACHER CAN DECIDE THE BEST WAY TO STOP BULLIES!!

★ When we feel hurt or scared by other kids that are stronger or older, we might feel like hurting them back. Please don't. BULLYING IS WRONG. DON'T BECOME A BULLY YOURSELF.

★ Sometimes what the bully says about us may sound like it's true and we feel badly about ourselves. It's okay to be different and look and feel different. We are all different in many ways. Be proud to be the way you are.

★ When another kid becomes a bully it means that kid has problems *and* needs help and possibly treatment. By telling the teacher you are *being* bullied, you are not only helping yourself, you are helping *everyone* in school and the bully as well.

★ If you are being bullied, don't forget, YOU ARE NOT ALONE! Everyone has been bullied at some point. Most children feel ashamed or scared to talk about it, so they keep it a secret.

★ If you are being bullied, remember, IT'S NOT YOUR FAULT! There is nothing you did or said. It's not about how you look or who you are. Bullies are people with problems.

Imagination

★ Howard tried to hurt the bullies in his imagination when he thought he was a Roborabbit with super powers. Using your imagination is fine and healthy. But in real life, if we are being bullied, we *need* to tell the teacher.

Little Voice in Our Heads

★ Sometimes we may hear a little voice in our head telling us the right thing to do. Another name for it is the "voice of reason" or "intuition." This little voice or intuition protects us and helps keep us safe. Just like Howard learned to listen to his teachers and his parents* and then to his heart**, in this book Howard learns how to listen to his little voice.

★ TO FEEL SAFE, HAPPY AND GOOD, LISTENING TO OURSELVES AND THOSE WE TRUST IS A MUST!

★ Howard did not want to listen to the voice right away. He was scared, and he did not want his friends to think he was a tattletale or snitch. When we listen to the voice of reason right away, we will stay out of a lot of trouble.

★ It may not be easy to listen to the little voice right away. PRACTICE AND YOU WILL GET BETTER AT IT!

Howard B. Wigglebottom Learns to Listen
** *Howard B. Wigglebottom Listens to His Heart*

Ideas to Encourage Children to Report Bullying

★ Create a bully box so children can leave an anonymous note about bullies.

★ Have a telephone number where a child can leave a message about bullies.

★ Choose a super kid of the week. Ask the child to fill in the blanks on a piece of paper. "Did you notice anyone being bullied this week?" "Did you bully anyone this week?"

To help make our schools safer, parents, educators, and therapists are invited to share their resources about bullying and their success stories. Please email them to info@wedolisten.com. We will add them to the existing list of bully resources at www.wedolisten.com.

To prevent and eradicate bullying, visit our
Solutions for Peace & Safety at Home and School page
@ www.wedolisten.com.

We offer free resources, guidelines, lessons, a poster and song.

Learn more about Howard's other adventures.

Books
Howard B. Wigglebottom Learns to Listen
Howard B. Wigglebottom Listens to His Heart

You may email the author at howardb@wedolisten.com

Comments and suggestions are welcome.